T0065508

Trapped Within Myself

ARL115

authorHOUSE®

AuthorHouse™
1663 Liberty Drive
Bloomington, IN 47403
www.authorhouse.com
Phone: 833-262-8899

Published by AuthorHouse 06/16/2021

ISBN: 978-1-6655-2873-3 (sc)
ISBN: 978-1-6655-2872-6 (e)

Print information available on the last page.

This book is printed on acid-free paper.

Contents

CHAPTER 1

Early Childhood Days

I am the fourth child of my parents. At this time, I had four brothers and no sister. Back in 1972, mama was eight months pregnant and was told she was having a girl. One day, she was hanging out clothes outside on the clothes line. During the argument something happen that caused mama to fall. I was so scared for her.

Every Friday, daddy gave mama money and then he would go out with his friends. They argued a lot, every week. Sometimes, I would sit on the floor underneath the dresser and put my hands over my ears to block out the arguing.

The very next month, mama went into labor. The labor was very intense for mama because the contractions had stopped. Her midwife, Mrs. Grand, was right there with her until she delivered. That evening we were told Betty was a still born or born dead. We got to see her lying on the bed fully dressed. She was such a beautiful baby and looked as if she was three to four months old and weighed over eleven pounds. They had her dressed in a diaper shirt and a cloth diaper.

My sister, Betty, death was devastating to all of us. Questions raced through my head as to why she was born this way. She laid in the bed for hours until the funeral home people came to get her.

Mama had taken out a hen out to cook earlier for supper. I hadn't never cooked on my own. I fried that hen and cooked something with it but I can't remember what it was. No one could eat that hen because I was told later that hens are not to be fried but boiled or baked. None of us had an appetite to eat anyway after being told our baby sister was born dead.

The arguments between my parents continued. I remember telling mama to leave him. She told me, "that sometimes you have to swallow some bitter pills". I didn't know what that meant at that time. Found out later in life that it meant that you have to take a lot or put up with a lot of stuff to keep peace and your family together.

Mama was fifteen years old when she married. I believe she was scared to leave him because he had taken care of her and her siblings after grand mama died.

We were told her mom (grandmama) died giving birth to her twin brother and sister. At that time my great grandmama raised them but after mama got married and great grandmother died, the two siblings; Reese and Reecee, stayed with her and daddy.

CHAPTER 2

Hospitalization with Pneumonia

---- ❈ ----

I remember I was around thirteen years old when I had pneumonia. I had been hurting for weeks in my side but I wouldn't tell mama. I didn't tell her because it came from my being rebellious by talking on the telephone in the wee hours of the morning with Kurk, dressing skimpy when it was cold outside and running outside barefoot. I did all these things in the cold. I knew I was sick and probably had something wrong with me but was too scared to tell mama.

One day the pain got so intense in my side and chest that I had to tell mama. Once I told her she took me to Dr. Bill's office for him to check me out. I had been running a fever and chills at times. Upon him examining me, he couldn't here but a little air going into my lungs after telling me to breathe in and out. He immediately told my parents that I was a very sick child. He instructed them to take me immediately to the hospital. He came right behind us almost beating us there. We went into the emergency room entrance where he told the nurses to get me into a room.

Before leaving the doctor office, he had told my parents I had pneumonia. He immediately took me into surgery because he said my lungs were full of cold and other fluids causing me to have chills, fever and the hurting of side and chest. At the hospital, they didn't have the equipment needed to do the surgery so he couldn't get the fluid off my lungs by making an incision in my left side to drain it off. He then told the paramedics to transport me by ambulance to the big hospital in Sunghill. By the time the ambulance arrived at the hospital, Dr. Bill pulled up too.

Dr. Bill went in giving orders telling them to start an IV., take me into surgery, what kind of procedure he wanted done and to call a lung specialist. Dr. Bill stayed right there to make sure I was taken care of. The staff there didn't know him nor had they seen him before. He really looked like a bomb off the street but when he cussed them out, they began to do as he requested. After the surgery, the hospital staff tried to put me in a semi-private room but Dr. Bill said "no". He made them put me in a private room. He said I had been through enough.

I didn't remember anything for about a week and a half. I barely remembered waking up and one day to hear mama say, "I love you and we are praying for you". That was the first time I remember hearing my parents say they loved me. I also remembered hearing voices in the room of mama talking with the doctors. I can't remember whether dad was there or not. I heard the doctor tell mama to come over near the door because they wanted to talk with her. They said, Mrs. Williams," we have done all we could do for me and all we could do now is pray".

I was lying there listening to them talk but couldn't respond to them. I remembered saying within myself, "I'm not going anywhere", meaning I wasn't going to die. Mama said that I was in a comma for about a week because I had been sick so long without telling anyone.

I stayed in the hospital for a month and a half (six weeks). When I came out of the coma, I was in an oxygen tent, tube running out my left side and tubes seem to be everywhere. Everyone was so glad I was doing better. It scared my parents because of what the doctors had told them about me not making it.

When the nurses came in to give me shots, they would ask where I wanted them to stick me, I just turned over and let them have the hip or butt. The staff were so nice to me and spoiled me. I would want ice cream, popsicles or whatever, they would get it from the refrigerator on the floor just to satisfy me.

I remembered Kurk coming to visit me while I was in the hospital but don't remembered what the conversation was about. Before then he would send word by mama telling them he wanted to see me.

It was the prayer of mama and others along with my determination within myself that kept me alive. By me dressing skimpy, being on the telephone early mornings and running outside barefoot in the cold caused me a lot of pain and almost death. God had a **plan** and **purpose** for my life although I didn't know him then, HE KEPT ME. I praise God for keeping me alive to preach, teach his gospel and help others to know him as my healer!

I remember sitting in the living room when adult movies were being shown. I start feeling uncomfortable because my body started feeling some type of way but couldn't talk with anyone about it. I thought I wasn't normal by feeling that way. After that, I became interested in boys but before that I was a tomboy. I grew up with nothing but brothers so I only had boys to play.

The boys were scared of me because I would act like Bruce Lee putting my hands on them, kicking, flipping them or running away from them. I also remember, I use to plait, braid and corn row my brothers' hair as well as other boys in the neighborhood. Our house was called the Sunday house and a lot of people came there young and old. A lot of boys would come up there to play with my brothers.

We weren't allowed to play after school nor weekends until our chores were done. Sometimes my brothers would get their friends to help out and that gave them more time to play. The boys kept the yard cleaned by raking and picking up things out the yard during the summer. During the winter, their jobs were to cut wood, pile it on the porch and from the porch to the living room to burn in the wood heater. They also washed dishes too.

5

My chores were to wash everybody clothes, hang them out on the line, take them in, fold them up and put them away. I also cooked and cleaned the house such as mopped, swept and picked up things off the floor. Mama taught me how to cook. Cooking was a daily routine for mom and me. Sometimes, I would make the fire in the heater or add wood to the fire.

At times I felt like Cinderella because I had to stay in the house doing all these things and seem like mama let my brothers do whatever. Don't get me wrong mama was a good mama but that's just how I felt at that time.

I remembered, when my brothers didn't wash dishes before going to bed, mama would wake them up in the middle of the night to make them wash them. Once I swept the clothes of my brothers out the door under the back doorsteps. I got tired of sweeping clothes from underneath their beds when it was time to wash. When mama found out what I had done, spanked me.

CHAPTER 3

First Miracle

❈

One Saturday morning, I was asleep in my bed and heard a very faint voice cry out saying "help me, help me". I jumped up out of bed trying to find out where the voice was coming from. I went to screen front door and saw daddy on one side and Billy on the other side of car and it looked as though they were trying to jack up the car. I asked them was everything alright and they both said the car had felled on Jackson.

Without hesitation, I ran to the front of the car to try and help them lift the car off of Jackson. I remember the car coming up and him rolling from underneath and coughing up blood. I remembered putting the car down and going back in the house.

Later on that same day, daddy and Billy were telling everybody how I came out and picked the car up off Jackson. It shocked me because I thought both of them were jacking up the car as I was approaching. They said that I was like super woman when I lifted the car by myself because neither one of them had their hands on it.

Ever since that day, Jackson tells me he owes me his life but I remind him that it was God who used me. I had no idea that God can use me as he did. God supernaturally used me, an instrument, to save a life. I know him to be a SAVIOR (saver).

CHAPTER 4

My First Love

--- ❈ ---

I felt in love with a boy name Philip and lost my virginity to him. He was very handsome and he ran track too. I was infatuated with him when he noticed me. Good looking, running track and interested in me, wow! I was tom boyish and didn't know a boy would like me as a girlfriend. He would ride his horse name "Solo" up to the house to visit with my brothers. I thought I wasn't that pretty for him to notice or pay attention to.

Eventually, we began talking, touching and then kissing. We would sneak away and go to the wooded area in the back of his parent's juke. We would make a bed of straw and we had intercourse. I remember him to be a great kisser. I would ask mama could I go to the "cave" which was the name of the juke in which he lived. His parents sold all kinds of candies and goodies there. This is how I would get to be with him without my parents knowing.

All the girls in the neighborhood was crazy about Philip because he was handsome and athletic. One day he told me, he was breaking up with me. I cried like a baby. Mama asked me what was wrong and I told her how he quit me. She said, "you will find you someone else.

There is more fish in the sea". I then told her, "I didn't want anyone else because I loved him".

I knew that he liked other girls but I didn't care as long as he was with me, sometimes. I didn't feel like I was good looking enough for any boy but when he noticed me, I felt good. He treated me good so I thought even though he was a track runner and well-known in community, school and he paid attention to me, that was something special.

CHAPTER 5

Other Guys in My Life

❈

Kurk stayed up the road from us. He started coming around or up to the house. He was older than I. We started talking, began spending time together at my house and with his family. He was a very quiet young man, smart and a gentleman. He loved to play with video games, go to the movies and pretty much home bodied.

I would sometimes play games with him at his house in his room. It was very boring to me because I wanted to do more than just play games. I wanted to party! One night Kurk drove up to the house to see me and saw Philip and I kissing. He just sat in the car and didn't say anything. I acknowledged him being there but I wanted to be with Philip. He and I weren't together but I loved him and wanted to be with him even for a second.

I knew Philip had other girlfriends but I was willing to share him as long as he would be with me from time to time. This hurt Kurk because he came to see me and saw me kissing my ex. Later on that week, I had to apologize to him and ask him to forgive me and he did.

I met another friend in the neighborhood named Johnathan, he was my second older brother age. I meet him at church. I remember him being kind and very sweet. He wanted to be my boyfriend but I really didn't like him like that. He took me to a football game one night and we just sat in the car and talked. He was the kindest and sweetest person you ever wanted to meet.

These two guys were awesome young men who never took advantage of me although I expected them too. All I wanted was to lay up with men, party and hangout. I didn't have girlfriends to hang out with like most girls my age.

My oldest brother set me up with an older guy and my daddy liked him because he would buy them beer and brought some each time he came to the house. I didn't feel comfortable sleeping around with this guy. He would give me money just to be with him at times and I didn't enjoy it at all.

I loved, trusted my brother and would have done anything for him. I was young, naive and thought sleeping around was everything. I would tell other girls now never do anything for someone else no matter who they were and what they would give you.

I realize that seeing adult movies triggered something within me that caused me to wonder what it would be like to do that. My curiosity got the best of me. Had me thinking that if I slept around that men would love and want to be with me. It just didn't work like that.

CHAPTER 6

My first Niece

❋

In 1975, my brother Fred and Ann had a little girl name Denise. That was our first niece and we all were crazy about her. Every weekend, we would go through the woods to get her and bring her to our house. We all spoiled her. She was my parents first grandchild as well as Ann's mother.

She was such a joy to have every week. I played with her, dressed, fed and took her outside often. The joy she put on all of our faces. Denise was like a baby doll but real. Fred and Ann got married on her mother, Michelle's porch while pregnant with Denise. It was a nice little ceremony and we all were happy for them.

Later on, Fred went to the army. We were all so proud of him. We wrote letters to each other often. I missed him a lot and considered him as my friend. He took care of his wife and child. Eventually, they both joined him when he got station after basic training.

CHAPTER 7

Blessed with Sister

In 1977, my sister, Christy was born. I was then 15 years old. I had prayed to God and told mama I wanted a sister. I remember one night, she kept crying and I took her out of the bed with my parents and after that she slept with me. My sister would get under my armpit every night and go to sleep.

Before my sister came along, my brother Donny was my "bae". He is two years younger than I am but Ben had to sleep in my bed because my other four brothers shared a bed. Now I had five brothers but Christy was our baby at that time. She was special to all of us.

When Fred went to the Army, Ben was able to move into the boys' room. Christy and I was able to have a room by ourselves. As time went by, I would write Fred because I missed him.

CHAPTER 8

Second Love

--- ❖ ---

Since I had only brothers for a long time, the boys in the community would come to our house to play. I would corn row, plait or braid the boy's hair in the community hair and also my brothers. Every Saturday, mama would go shopping but this particular Saturday, my oldest brother called James and told him to come up there since my parents were gone. I was in bed asleep and I felt someone over me. I looked up to see James right in my face. I pushed him away and told him to leave me alone. He kept bothering me.

One day, on a Saturday, he was called up there again, I pushed him away, we wrestled and began kissing. After that, we began liking each other. Every day he would come up to the house to see my brothers but actually to see me. We began having intercourse almost nightly. He started saving me a seat on the bus when we went to school because I was his girlfriend. He was a loud mouth person and at first I didn't like him because he was too loud and talked all the time.

I remember my sister sitting in between us when James tried to get close to me. She loved herself some James because he took up time with her by playing with her. Sometimes he would put her to sleep. He even taught her how to dance on his shoulders. She would always be in my arms when he came to see me.

After about two years of having intercourse, I got pregnant. I remembered him asking me what I wanted for my sixteen birthday and told him a baby. Strangely enough I was already pregnant with our first born.

I was due to have Dewayne that following April 1979. I was afraid to tell mama I was pregnant but by her and I cooking together, we would bump into one another while in the kitchen. She sensed something was wrong with me. My stomach was hard and mama knew because I would rub against her in passing, while in the kitchen. One day in kitchen she asked me was I pregnant. I bucked my shoulders at first like I didn't know. I admitted I was but she already knew.

That year mama, the hog, the dog and I were all pregnant. Each month, thereafter was a new addition to the family. I believe, I started off in April and mama finished off in August 1979 with my baby brother.

Some of mama friends were scaring me up saying that the baby was going to burst my tail open. Mama talked with me and told me if I just do what the midwife tell me, I would be find. I remembered having my first born, Dewayne, on April 4, 1979, he was a beautiful baby weighing right at seven pounds. My midwife, Mrs. Grand, assisted me with the birth at home. I had my baby in my bed and the fee for delivery was $50.00.

James was in living room when I was in labor and stayed until I delivered. We were proud parents for the first time. He would be eighteen that October and I would be seventeen in September of that year.

Dewayne was Charlotte's first grandchild. He was spoiled by the whole family including great grandma, Mrs. Ruth and great granddaddy, Steven. They began taking him home with them before he was six months old. He was a chubby and handsome baby. At that time, he had four generations on both side of the family.

CHAPTER 9

Graduation Night

When I graduated from high school, I was already three months pregnant with Rodney. No one came to my graduation. Mama and daddy said they couldn't find anyone to bring them. James was supposed to go with me but got his sister, Carol, to drop me off. I felt so alone! After graduation was over, my classmates were going out to celebrate at the club but I caught a ride and went home.

After arriving home, I felt more miserable because everyone was sitting around drinking, laughing and not paying any attention to me. I went straight to bed and cried. I cried for hours that night, soaking both sides of my pillow until I went to sleep. I was mad with everyone including myself. This was supposed to be a happy time in my life because I graduated. James didn't show up (my children's dad and the love of my life) and none of my family. I kept asking myself, "What did I do so wrong for nobody to come to my graduation"?

It seems at that time that no one but Dewayne, my baby boy, loved me. I felt so bad inside like I could just crawl up in a hole. Now pregnant with my second son and no one cared. I said to myself, at least my children will love and need me.

CHAPTER 10

James Left Me

James left me for a girl name Jade that came to town who he met at the club. He was the disc jockey at that time. He got involved with her, she told him all kinds of things she would do for him and he felled for it. One night, I was at James' house and I got mad with him and asked him to take me home but he wouldn't. I called Kurk to pick me up and take me home. Charlotte, James' mother, along with his sisters, got mad with me for doing this and told him that the baby I was carrying wasn't his but it was Kurk's.

I knew that was a lie because James had been the only guy I had intercourse with three years. Later on he began to come around less and less. When he did come around, he just wanted to sleep around. This particular night, we were having a discussion and he told me that the baby I was carrying was not his. I told him that that wasn't true.

He was the only one I had been with and how could he even think of me as being low down that I would put a baby on him if it wasn't his. I cried like a baby that night as well soaking my pillow with tears because I was so hurt.

I later found out that the reason he said the baby wasn't his was to hurt me so it would be easier for him to move to Winfield with this girl he met. After a couple of days, he began calling me wanting to talk and to tell me how much he missed me. He said that Jade had promised him that she was going to throw a big party for him and introduce him to her friends. She was going to take care of him. After throwing the party, she changed, he said. She left him with her two boys while she went to work. He was the babysitter and wasn't allowed to go anywhere unless she took him.

She locked him up along with her boys daily and he was on lock down. He got tired of the situation quickly. He wanted to come home. Of course, I still loved him and told him we can try our relationship again. Now he had to figure out how he would escape from the eleventh floor to catch a bus back home. He knew the time she was to arrive home and he stood at the door with his bag and waited for her to open the door. As soon as she did, he pushed her aside to get out and get on the elevator. She got on the elevator also and they fought all the way down to the ground floor.

He was trying to get away and had to leave with only the clothes on his back. When he got to Hapview, he caught a ride to Manscester and was put off side the road and came through the pasture in front of my house to me. He was so stank and hungry. He had ridden the bus a long way home. He only had the one set of clothes and that was what he was wearing. I fixed him something to eat, he laid across my bed and went to sleep. He said that he hadn't slept nor ate in about two days and just wanted to get home.

The relationship wasn't the same thereafter. He continued to be with other females, spent less and less time with me and our baby. I can't remember where he was when our second child was born. He later found out I had the baby but he still didn't come around as much. He really believed that the baby wasn't his.

Charolette started getting Dewayne when he was a month old. That was her first grandchild. All of them had him spoiled. When Rodney came along, it was a different story. Charlotte would say, "I'll get Rodney when he gets older and out of diapers because I can't handle the both of them". He would cry to go with her and she always had an excuse. I would just hold him and love on him, tell him it wasn't his fault because his grandma wouldn't take up time with him.

I accepted James no matter who he dated or had relations with because I just wanted him. My self –esteem was very low thinking that no one else wanted me. I would tell him as long as he was happy, I was happy. Didn't know that, that was a lie from the pits of hell until now. I allowed a lot of craziness to happen during our relationship.

CHAPTER 11

Moved to Emerald

--- ✖ ---

Rodney was three months old when James asked me to move to where he was and we were to get married. Well, I did move to Emerald in February 1981 along with our two boys. James had already got us a house to stay in. We stayed around the road from Uncle Daniel's barbershop. I just wanted to be with the man I loved in hopes to be his wife.

His grandparents, Mr. Steven and Mrs. Ruth took us to where he lived. I was eighteen years old when I left home for the first time. James was working in construction with his Uncle Sammy. He would get home close to dark every evening. I remember not having a television but only a radio in the house. I would listen to music every day on the country station because that's all I could pick up at that time.

I knew no one but James, Uncle Daniel and Uncle Sammy. In a strange place and didn't know anyone that I could talk with or visit. I believe I might have been there for about a week in a half when a girl came to the front door asking for James. When he got home that evening, I told him he had a visitor. I saw another girl walking by when I was at the back door open. She came on the porch, knocked and asked for him. She told me her name but I don't remember it.

When James came home, I told him that he had another visitor. I told him to let everyone know that his wife was in town and for them to not come to his house anymore. Even on the weekends, he would go out, leave home and will be gone for hours at a time.

I had gotten lonely being in a strange town with my two babies and nowhere to go. I had to wash clothes in the bathtub because we didn't have a washer nor dryer. I began to complain and tell him if he didn't spend time with us that I was going back home. I told him he had lied to me concerning marrying me. He tried to assure me that he was going to marry me but not right now.

I felt he wanted to play the field by having a woman at home who could cook and take care of the children while he still lived a single lifestyle. So I called home and told daddy to come get us. He didn't exchange words. This particular morning, I heard daddy voice. He was next door asking the neighbor did they know me. I jumped out of bed, went on the porch and told them they were at the wrong house. They arrived early that Monday morning before daybreak and before James went to work. He asked me why where they there and I told him that me and the children were going back home. He pleaded for me to stay but my mind was made up.

Once he got home from work, he called me. He said he wished that I would have talked to him before I left. I told him he was never there to talk to because he came home late. By the time I put the children to bed, I was tired and worn out. It was a job with two babies, washing clothes in the bath tub, hanging them around the house and making sure they were taken care of and also having his food prepared when he got home.

CHAPTER 12

James Returning to Manscester

━━━━━━━━━━━━━ ❖ ━━━━━━━━━━━━━

A couple of months later James moved back home to Manscester, I thought, to be with me and the boys. He always had other girls in his life. He called himself a gigolo, partying, drinking and making out with other females.

My daddy would allow James to go see other girls in his truck. I was so hurt by that. I held that in my heart for years before I was able to confront him about what he had done and how I felt about it. I just felt like all the men in my life was hurting me intentionally. I loved both of them but didn't trust them. James and my relationship was rocky after conception with Rodney. I didn't date nor have intimate relationship with anyone for a long time.

I decided to go back to school and take up a trade. I would walk out to elementary school and catch the van to school and back. I thought I looked cute in my white dress, white stocking and white shoes. I received a Nursing Aide certificate in 1982 at the vocational school in Sunghill.

James and I still dated off and on. We had sex in the living room on the chair in my parents' house. I got pregnant with our daughter. When I told mama and daddy about the third pregnancy, daddy got his shot gun and went around the road to find James. I was crying telling daddy not to shoot him because it took the both of us and that I loved him. He still went looking for him but didn't find him at that time.

I met Chris through Kurk while pregnant with my daughter. We began dating and told him I was pregnant but he still wanted to be with me. He was a nice, tall and dark young man. That boy could sing love songs like Luther and Teddy. He spent a lot of time with the boys and I.

Twanna was delivered March 1984 and James wasn't around when she was born. His mother had to tell him, he had a daughter. His mother actually went to the hospital with me. Our daughter was the only child I had at the hospital because of some female issues and doctor recommended it.

I continued to date Chris and after two months, we became intimate. He was very good to my children and me. He would buy us things even though my children weren't his. That relationship didn't last long because he wasn't interested in me anymore.

Chris and I was off and on in our relationship. I had seen other guys after Twanna was born but mainly to have someone in my life. I began dating married and single men, father and son just to not be alone and experiencing intercourse with different people.

I just felt as long as I had something in my life, I was loved, wanted or even needed. Didn't know that I wasn't that person who I looked at in the mirror. Yes, there was some good intercourse but it wasn't who I was. That's all I knew, was to sleep around. I got tired of making excuses to be with them or not to be with them and dodging them.

Somewhere down the line, I got hooked back up with James but this time I was ready for a commitment. We talked about our three kids we had together and seem like he kept coming back.

In August 1984, I began working at State Hospital temporary as a Human Service Worker I (nurse assistant). I continued to apply for full time positions and finally got on as a custodial worker.

I loved my job cleaning in unit. My job was to vacuum the offices, take out trash, clean bathrooms outside of the ward, sweep, mop, buff outside halls and dining room on the fourth floor in the unit. After about eight months, I wanted to work in field in which I was certified. I went back to Park Trammel, Unit 16, working with the elderly clients.

My daughter, Twanna, was six months old when I began work and mama kept all three of my children while I worked. I worked the 3-1130 p.m. shift. I rode the van from Manscester to Borough daily until I was able to buy me a car.

CHAPTER 13

Moving into my First Place

I had moved out of my parents' home at age twenty-five years old. My brother, Donny, had gone to the army. Before he went to the army, he was buying the single-wide mobile home with two bedrooms. After being in the service for a while, he told me that if I took up the payments that I could move in his mobile home. He didn't think he would be coming back for a long time.

Daddy knew this man who loaned out money who could help me to get the mobile home. Donny had told me that I could trade it in for something bigger since I had three kids. My daddy talked with this man, Mr. Adams, because he also had real estate property. He could get me into a double wide and get someone to take over payments on the single wide. It was a deal!

The single wide got moved and a double wide, 1971, three bedrooms, two full baths was put in its place. Daddy and mama signed the land over to me for collateral so I could get the loan. My children and I moved into the trailer in July 1987. James moved in as well because he wanted to be with us.

I told him I didn't want to shack up. The saying, "Why buy the cow when the milk is free" kept ringing in my head. He wasn't working at the time. He had always worked since he dropped out of school in the eleventh grade but he wasn't at that time. I told him he can either marry me or go back home with his mother.

We decided to get married. We sat the date for September 1987. Since he wasn't working, we went to the flea market in Sunghill and I bought rings for the both of us. I made the cake, blue and white for our reception. I paid the preacher and did all the fixings for the reception. We got married in his grandparents' yard and his best friend, Jackson, who the car had felt on was his best man. The wedding was during the family reunion on his side of the family.

Twanna was three years old, Rodney was seven years old and Dewayne was eight years old when we got married September 1987. It was a hot day that day. A couple of my family members were there but not a whole lot. After the wedding, we stayed awhile to the family reunion but later went home and had a little reception at our mobile home. Things were going well for a while. James later got a job as a brick mason. He was making twelve dollars an hour. Sometimes his boss wouldn't pay him on Friday and had to find him to get paid.

God had allowed me to buy James a blue Chevy truck from Jerry. We had two vehicles, trailer, three kids and each other. James worked in the day and I worked evening shift at hospital in Borough.

I remembered one Christmas, we had made plans to buy the kids Christmas. That Friday, Tyler failed to show up with the checks. James was really, really mad with him. The children didn't have the Christmas we wanted for them but we were still able to buy some toys. James also became a disc jockey (DJ) at his cousin club around the road. He would come home, change clothes and go DJ on Friday through Sunday nights.

I would be left home with the children all the time. I became depressed and lonely. One day, I was driving home and said to myself "just drive and keep driving and leave it all behind". I then thought of my kids. Told myself no one would treat my children like I wanted them to be treated or love them the way I could. So I kept going back home remaining in the relationship that I wasn't comfortable nor satisfied with anymore.

I began committing adultery, partying and drinking, from Thursday through Sunday nights. I partied and were doing things I didn't like but I was trying to find love, compassion and whatever else I thought I needed. I had been faithful and did all I knew to do to please my husband to keep our family together and be happy. I would tell myself and James, as long as he was happy, I was happy. That was the biggest lie I could have ever told. I was not happy and I was miserable, lonely, stupid and tired.

I began seeing a psychological counselor because I wasn't functioning well on my job nor at home. When I told my children about it, they ask me was I crazy. I told them I just needed help and needed someone to talk to. I would go once a week to see Mrs. Victoria, my counselor. She was so sweet and helpful. She would allow me to come and just spill my guts out to her. I knew each time I went to my meetings that I would be able to speak freely and not be criticize.

Mrs. Victoria would listen and ask me questions as to how can I change the circumstance or situation. She would allow *me* to come up with *my* own strategy of solving *my* own problems. I went to counseling for over a year but when I stopped going to her, I had a new perspective on life. She was a life saver. My insurance at the beginning did not pay for my sessions but she still allowed me to come any way. God gave me favor with Mrs. Victoria to get my life back on track and to live life to the fullest. I'm glad I made a choice to do right and to seek help or counsel when I needed it.

James had gotten hurt from falling off the scaffold while working laying bricks and popped his back. I had to go to emergency room where they had taken him. He was in so much pain and wrapped his arms around my waist crying like a baby. He thought he would never walk again or function because of the accident. I was working 3p.m.- 11 p.m. shift at hospital. Mama took care of him when I went to work.er while I was there. She would make sure he had food, water, assisted him to bathroom when needed.

Charlotte after she got off from work, her and mama would see that he had what he needed until I got home at night. For months, he wasn't able to work at all. His back did get better and he returned back to work. Since he got hurt on the job he received a settlement in 1991 and paid off the mobile home.

During the time he got the settlement, he starting doing crazy things with money. I remember him renting a car one weekend when he already had a car. He wouldn't allow me to drive the car but allowed a friend of his, Henry, to drive. I was very upset with him because he was wasting money and being irresponsible. He was going more, spending money and partying like tomorrow wasn't coming. That really drew a bigger wedge in our relationship.

In 1992, I decided to go back to school and take up another trade at a vocational school. I attended for a year and was going from 8 a.m. – 12 noon and worked from 3:00 p.m. to 11:30 p.m. I received my certificate March 1993 for a Word Processing System Operator.

In March 1995, James and I got a divorce and I paid for it. It went well. He didn't object to anything. Since I had financed the marriage, I also financed the divorce too. I had gone to the courthouse and got the papers. Once I filled them out, I submitted them and it didn't take long for the divorce to be finalized. The children had told me before the divorce was final that they wanted me to keep my married name it was their last name. I didn't have a problem with that.

CHAPTER 14

My Life Changed

When I was going out partying, I found myself falling asleep at the table. I didn't want to drink, dance nor talk to men anymore. Ann and I would sit at the table almost bumping heads falling asleep while in the club. I would say to myself, I would sit in church or at the juke thinking, why am I here? It had to be more to life than this.

Before I got saved that year, I was still attending my family church, the church I grew up in. I found myself going to church falling asleep after the choir sang. I didn't quite know what was happening but felt I was there in body but not in spirit and knew a change had to come. I talked to dad about how I felt God was telling me to leave the church. He told me that if God told me that then I should do what he says.

In the year of 1995, a friend name, Sharon, invited me to church. She told me about the evangelist from south Curtail rendering services in the panhandle. I started going to the service. The services were different than I was accustomed to. I continued to go and before long, I got saved in August of that same year. I really loved the woman of God.

I got to know her personally. We would go to her home sometimes for cookout in Greenfield. We would keep in touch with each other outside of church as well. The services were good and informative. I heard the word preached different than at my church. I learned a lot from the ministry. Every time she would come to the panhandle, I was in church and I followed her for three years.

One night, I had a dream that I was at church with Evangelist Sarah ministering and there was a petition between us. I was behind the petition. I could hear her voice but couldn't see her. A lot of screeching voices, high pitched was heard. She wrote something on a sheet of paper and was passing it around the room.

When the paper reached me, there wasn't anything on it. I kept thinking about the petition separating us. After pondering within myself, a petition means separation. I still continued to go to church anyhow. Things really got crazy. I began to hear her say things that wasn't biblical but worldly. I began seeing things that I knew wasn't right. I kept hearing in my head, separation, separation! I finally got it. I ask God to send me somewhere where a man or woman of God wasn't just preaching the word but living, walking, talking and doing the word of God.

In 1996, my best friend, Ann had divorce my oldest brother and remarried on the same day. I got call and was asked to stop by her house. After arriving to her house, she told me she had married John. I wanted her to be happy so I said if the Lord told you both to do this then I am happy for you.

Later on when I visited her, I wasn't allowed to come into house. When I tried to talk with her, she held her head down with no eye contact and didn't talk to me because her husband was right there. After several attempts, stopping by her house to talk with her and communication was cut completely off.

That was very devastating to me because we had been friends since we were teenagers. I lost my best friend to a man that had dishonest gain of her life and the children. Found out that he knew she was vulnerable and used the word of God to entice and marry her. She nor the children were allowed to speak with her family, my family nor friends but only his.

Years past and I learned to move on through keeping myself involved in church. Never had experience so much pain of losing someone who was alive but yet dead to me. I then began putting a wall up and not letting anyone else get that close to me.

One night I went to Pastor Sarah service again and Ann was there. She knew we had been friends for a long time and made us hug each other but Ann was reluctant in hugging me. She still didn't acknowledge our friendship and that I still loved her as my sister. The hug was cold and nothing had changed at that point in my life regarding her, my friend.

I know now the only thing kept me alive and focus was the grace of God. He kept me from being bitter toward her and the situation. There were times I would pick up the phone to call her but knew that I wouldn't get an answer. I just stayed in the word of God and in church.

CHAPTER 15

Joined Trinity Deliverance and Restoration Center

❈

The latter part of 1997, my same friend, Sharon, invited me once again to another church name, Pastor Yvette was the pastor, under the leadership of Pastor Nico. I attended this church several times in December 1997 and in January 1998. I enjoyed the services very much although I didn't understand their praise and worship.

Elder Rebecca and Pastor Simon rendered services because the pastor of the church was sick and in the hospital during that time. I felt when they ministered, they ministered went straight to my heart. I felt at home with such a peace I never felt before. I was searching for a church home. God had me on a mission.

In February of 1998, I went to church again this particular Sunday, I finally saw the Pastor of the church. She was ministering that morning. She called me out and asked me to stand up. As I was standing, she began to minister to me. She said, "As you were standing up, I saw you being shot out of a canon. God says he is going to shoot you up fast. He says, you got to get rooted and grounded first".

I knew that very instant I was to join that church and needed a church home. I had already prayed about it before that Sunday. I joined the church under **watch care** and been a member ever since.

Sometime later, the church split and Pastor Yvette named the church Trinity Deliverance and Restoration Center. She had Pastor Al drew up papers and she rename the church and became pastor of it.

In September of that same year, I drove to Truehill with Pastor Yvette and Twanna. We went to a well-known ministry under the leadership of Pastor Silas. I hadn't traveled that far before. I stayed at home with the children and my family. It was a great experience for me. The drive was long but I enjoyed experiencing a Holy Ghost filled atmosphere.

I remember us standing in line waiting to get in the evening service. It was kind of hot outside. The people began to just praise and worship God. The anointing was high. When one person stop singing, someone else began. It was just awesome! We finally made it inside the building. It was so huge and flags were on all walls representing different countries. The staff were friendly. We met a lot of people mostly pastors from all over the universe. Pastor Jack joined the Ministerial Fellowship and I joined as a partner.

At that time, we traveled to Truehill in my red Dodge Neon which had a front oil seal leak. We only had fifty dollars for gas. We were determining to go, so we filled the car up and stepped out on faith. The word of God says as you go, he will bless you. People bought us food and all our needs were met and we came back home safely without any problems.

On our way back from Truehill, Pastor Yvette told me that she wanted me to be the praise team leader. I question it time and time again but I had said whatever my Pastor ask me to do I will do it to the best of my ability.

I knew nothing about picking songs, range of voices, how to lead or anything. The praise team gave me a hard time. I told them from the beginning I didn't know what I was doing. Some of them got frustrated. I became frustrated myself because I didn't have no clue as to what I was doing.

Pastor Yvette and I became close. She told me that Twanna couldn't go on trips with us anymore because it cost more. I didn't like what she said but it did make since. Instead of two people having to buy for it would have been three. If I wasn't at her house, she would come to my house. We talked everyday as well. My life wasn't my own anymore and my family really didn't understand and didn't like it. They thought she had roots or something on me. She took up a lot of my time and they really didn't like that at all.

The members at church began to talk to me about Pastor Yvette individually. They wanted me to take sides with them because they knew her. All I know was God had sent me there and I was there for the pastor not so much for them. When the church had split a couple months before then, I left as well. I had just got there so I felt, I had nothing to lose. I left with the majority. It bothered me because I was back where I started without a church home. Pastor Jack called me several times to check on me and to tell me God loved me and so did she.

I began to play that in my mind over and over. I felt the Holy Spirit telling me to go back. He said, "You told me to send you to a place where the man or woman of God is preaching, teaching and living my word". Go back with your tail tucked in all. Don't be ashamed. I put you there for the pastor and you must lift her up. Pray for her! Anything you see in her that is not right, bring it to me and I will change her or the situation. I went back to Trinity and never left again. I have a mandate on my life to continue in the ministry and do all I can for pastor and be obedient to God's spirit.

Most of the people had left the church but those who followed Pastor Yvette remained. We had about five families there including Mother Sealy, the eldest. There were some trying times but God always seem to come through for the congregation.

We traveled to several ministries in Curtail, Weecha, Truehill and many other places. We went to Bashville at least twice a year.

I was the praise team leader, the house keeper, the prayer warrior, the armor bearer, the finance person, bill payer, program maker, holiday planner and everything else I needed to be. Pastor Yvette would ask others to do different tasks but they wouldn't do it. She began calling on me more and more because she knew I would get it done. Sometimes, I would get overwhelmed. I ask God to give me strength to do all that was on my plate.

I remember one night during prayer at church, I was on my knees asking God to forgive me for my many mistakes. This particular night, an older lady came to me after prayer and asked if she could say something to me. I listen to her and was told that God said he had forgiven me the moment I asked him to but now I needed to forgive myself.

I had also told God "yes" to his will and "yes" to his way. Told God, that I'll go if I have to go by myself. There were times I was literally by myself. No praise team members showed up for rehearsal or Sunday morning service. I had to do praise and worship alone. I was terrified and nervous but I did my best and that is what God requires, **our best**. They began to call me Pastor Yvette pet. That I was a gopher. She liked me better than them. Telling me all sorts of things concerning her.

I almost left the ministry again but I thought about the mandate God had given me. He placed me in the ministry for the pastor not for them. My job was to keep her prayed up and be there for her. Whatever she needed, I was to help her physically, financially or whatever else needed. God had truly blessed me through my obedience to him. I have learned how to take a licking and keep on ticking. My trials and tribulations hasn't been easy but fruitful. I've learned so much in my saved life.

Anything I found to do at church, I would do it without asking questions or thinking of the cost. I made sure the bathroom was clean, sanctuary was clean and fresh, floors, office, sound booth was dusted. I even bought groceries for two members of the church and also Pastor Jack at times without looking for them to repay me. I love helping people.

CHAPTER 16

Second Miracle

In February 2001, Saturday evening before my first speaking or trial sermon that Sunday, both my brothers got electrocuted in the yard. This day I was getting my hair done at my trailer when I heard a loud noise outside. I rose up from my chair to see what was going on. I saw a lot of people gathered in the yard and from a distance saw my two brothers on the ground. Donny was bleeding from temple and Billy was held up by Fred, my oldest brother.

I looked at both my brothers and thought that Donny was hurt more because I saw blood on his face. I began to pray for him but he told me it was just a cut from a tire rim he hit when he felled to the ground. He then told me to see about baby brother. When I arrived to feel baby brother arm, it felt calamity and sort of cold. His body laid in Fred's arm hanging over like a puppet or dish rag as if he was dead. I began to pray and remember saying "you will live and not die". After repeatedly saying these words, he sneezed and not long after that he opened his eyes and began crying.

By this time, the ambulance had come. The paramedics was checking both of them. They asked what had happened. Apparently dad had them checking the well because something was wrong with the water. When they both lifted up the iron pole to put it down in the well, it touched the main electrical wire and caused the electricity to come down the pole which they both were holding, knocking them both to the ground.

Since Billy was taller than Donny, he was hit by more electricity. The electricity went through baby brother body out of the back of his foot embedding (melting) the plastic sandals into the heel of his foot. He was taken by ambulance to the hospital in Scotty and mama went with him. Donny was alright and didn't have to go to hospital.

The next day, I had my first speaking (trial sermon) at Trinity Deliverance and Restoration Center. My topic was "**For Such a Time as This**" from the book of Esther. A few of my family members were there but mom was with my baby brother. My oldest brother, Fred, had said that Saturday after everything had happen, that I had already preached after witnessing me laying hands on baby brother and life came back in his body. I know Jesus raised the dead as he did Lazarus.

I really didn't know what or how God use me the second time. He was showing me and others that he still works miracles through signs and wonders. For me, I was still stunned and at awe how this big God can use this frail and insecure girl from Manscester, Wow!

CHAPTER 17

Experiences in other Ministries

❖

I've seen so much in ministries. Some real and some unreal. People are ignorant because of their lack of knowledge. Before I left Evangelist Sarah ministry, God allowed me to hear some things. The things which I heard wasn't holy. I heard her say that if someone pissed on the floor what she would do to them. She said the "...it" word one night. This woman got upset one night over money (offering).

It's a lot took place after God had told me to separate from that ministry. When you are out of the will of God, he began to show you things or allow you to hear things. I was very hurt but God kept me through it all. You need to obey immediately when he tells you to do something. Don't try to understand or figure it out, just do it!

One night I went to a revival at a liquor store off of the parkway. The liquor store had closed so this prophetess and her husband opened it as a church. During the revival, they tried to cast a demon out of a woman. The demonic spirit within her caused her to slide across the floor when the prophetess and other men of God tried to cast it out. I was pleading the blood of Jesus because that wasn't what I was taught when Jesus and others cast evil spirits out of people in the bible. I was taught that the spirit could leave a person and jump into someone else if it wasn't handled properly.

I just wasn't taking any chances. As I was observing, I said to myself this is wrong. I thought it was me at the time but it was holy spirit speaking to me telling me that. I hadn't read in the bible where they kept repeating over and over again for the demon to come out. My bible tells me that Jesus said "Come out" and immediately the demon(s) left that person in whom they were in.

Occasionally, I would go to hear Evangelist Craft when she came to Hapview rendering services. She would always say the Lord say, "if you put twenty, fifty or a hundred dollars in an envelope, God would bless you". If it's a car you want, family member saved or whatever you're asking for that you should sow a seed to meet that need. It will happen in a certain amount of time or days.

I kept going back before I realize this wasn't of God. God don't ask you to give money to receive a blessing from him. God will give you your heart's desire if you are faithful and obedient to his word. You can't pay God enough to receive a blessing from him. He blesses you because he loves you.

I was asked to preach at a church who was having a Fruit of the Spirit program. Everyone on the program was only to speak for seven minutes. Found out later that the program was to raise money for the church. I never did that again. Pastor Jack always taught us that if someone wants you to preach, let you be the keynote or main speaker for that time. We don't want to be out of the will of God by preaching for money.

Don't allow people to pump you up by telling you you've done a good job. Always give the glory to God! I remember my friend who invited me to go to different churches had me to preach for her one Friday night. I asked Pastor Jack was it alright to go. She blessed me and I took some of the members with me for support. Afterwards she told me how God used me, just for a moment, I said thank you and began to feel good about myself. Pastor Jack had reminded me before then that people will *flatter* you with words but you must always remain humble. Give God all the glory and praise.

CHAPTER 18

Moved to Hapview

─────────── ❈ ───────────

In the latter part of 2003, I moved from my trailer to a duplex in Hapview. Pastor Yvette had told me about the vacant apartment and talked with her sister about renting it out to me and she agreed. I was mad with my parents, fed up and wanted to leave from around them.

My children, at times, would tell me that my parents were talking about me in front of them. I didn't know how to confront them on what was told instead I just allowed anger to build up in me. It had got to the point; I didn't want to live there anymore.

After hearing what was said about me, I cried many nights soaking my pillows and wondering why they would do that especially in front of my children. I do remember one day saying something to mama about what they say hurt people feeling. She told me I say what I want to because I am grown. This had been going on for several years before I just left.

At that time when I moved, Twanna was a teenager but wasn't sure where she wanted to be. She was in and out the house so therefore, I felt there was nothing to stay in Manscester for anyway.

I moved into a two-bedroom duplex and didn't tell mama nor daddy I was moving. They saw the truck backed up to the back door.

I gathered all my stuff I wanted to take and left there hurt and sad. Twanna did stay with me sometimes but wasn't there most of the time. It was so peaceful in the apartment.

Dewayne wanted to know my whereabouts so he bought my first cell phone. He would call me checking in or I would call him to ask where he was. We would say "10-4" or "roger that". It was pretty cool having him call on a regular basis checking on me and I looked forward to it. He would come over to my apartment at times just to lay his head in my lap, fall asleep or other times wanting his hair braided, permed or both.

After being in the apartment for a while, I found out that Sealy, my friend, had had a stroke. She was staying with her mother who was up in age and couldn't help her. She wasn't able to stay there needing therapy and someone to do for her. I told her that she could move in with me after getting approval from my landlord. I would be there for her and it was more convenient for her therapist to come there.

I was still working so myself along with her made an agreement that her children can come over some days to visit her. This would ensure someone there with her and also for therapist to come in and do whatever she needed done. Shirley children started leaving their kids and she had to babysit them. I had problems with that because she was sickly herself.

After Susie telling me about her mom having mold in her mobile home. I asked the landlord was it alright for Susie mother to move there and they pay rent. She agreed to them renting the duplex.

The early part of 2005, I felt the Lord was telling me to move in with Pastor Yvette. My family wasn't too crazy about Pastor Yvette. I didn't care what my family was saying at that time and knew to be obedient to the voice of God.

I had already told pastor about I felt God had told me to move in with her and she agreed. I moved in with her and Leroy. It was alright but my driving from her house to work was a bit of a stretch. I was given the bedroom that her sister Ann had died in. I was afraid to go to sleep in the room when I first moved there but it became peaceful after praying.

Dewayne had told me that he wasn't coming to visit as long as I was staying with her. That hurt me but I understood and would stop by after work to see him in Manscester. We still would talk on the phone but it wasn't the same after I moved in with Pastor Jack. She did welcome my family to her house but only Twanna would come.

CHAPTER 19

Son Murdered

---— ❈ ——---

On March 2005, I went by the house where I raised my children in our 1971 mobile home in Manscester to see my son, Dewayne. I remember seeing him that evening standing in front door of trailer smoking a cigarette. It was a Tuesday evening after work, I stopped by to see him. He was upset because his baby granddaddy, Sweet, wouldn't allow him to see his four-month old baby boy. I tried to encourage him and told him that he will see his baby soon. Didn't know that he wouldn't. He seemed alright when I left him that evening!

That Wednesday, of March 2005, while at work, received several phone calls left on my office phone. I had taken several clients out shopping in Maitland, Louise and I. Once we got back from shopping to the ward, the ward supervisor came up to me telling me there had been an emergency call for me and I needed to call my daddy as soon as possible. I first had to get the van unloaded of the client's belongings and take them to rehabilitative room to be inventoried.

After doing that, I went to office to listen at messages. My brother, Ricky, from Miami had left message on phone telling me about Dewayne had got shot. I then called daddy and he confirmed it and that I needed to get home soon as possible. It was very hard for me to believe my son had been shot.

I then told the ward staff and Louise, the rehab staff and friend what had happen. She signed out to go with me. She seemed more upset that I. I then left heading to Manscester and Louise rode with me. I got to daddy house and he told me they were around the road in the field. Once I arrived down the dirt road, I saw a lot of people lingering in the streets. I parked the car and began walking toward crowd asking where Dewayne was and I wanted to see him.

While driving from work to Manscester, all I could think about was if I could get to him and lay my hands on him, he would live like God allowed my baby brother to live. After arriving there, James and Mary had made it as well, Twanna was crying loud and Rodney hadn't got there yet. So I told Thomas when he sees Rodney to catch him because I knew he was going to be very upset and want to kill someone about his brother.

Police escorted us close to the crime scene and put us on a bus with the immediate family and told me that we would be able to see him but that was a lie. We waited for hours before they told us we couldn't see him in the crime scene because we could tamper with the evidence. They had a pastor come on the bus to pray with the family but by that time, I didn't want to hear no prayer, I just wanted to see my son.

It was a big mess that evening, they sent us home after homicide had come on the scene and evidence had been gotten. We all went to the house but my other son, Rodney, Billy, Thomas and a couple others boys wanted to find the dude they say killed Dewayne. Somehow, the boys loaded up the car and went looking for the person without our knowledge. I prayed and told God to protect them and that I didn't want another killing that night. The Sheriff upon talking with us said that they will get him that night.

If I remember correctly before 10 p.m. that night, we received a call that they had arrested the boy. That was a relief for the family because the young people family and friends of Dewayne wasn't going to rest that night knowing his killer wasn't locked up. People were still at daddy's house but I lived with Pastor Yvette. I was tired and worn, just wanted to go home and get in my bed.

Once I got there, I went straight to my room. Told Pastor Yvette what had happen when she came to room. I just cried on her shoulder for a while because it hurt me to know my son had been murdered. I really didn't sleep much that night and went to work the next day. My client's had done a poster board telling me that they were sorry for what had happen to my son and several of them signed their names.

The staff on the ward was trying to console me and asked me what was I doing back at work when this had just happen to my son. I stayed in my office most of the day because that was my safe haven to cry and listen to praise and worship songs. I believe I did take the rest of the week off to make funeral arrangements for my son which was held that Saturday.

In June 2005, I retired from the hospital after working there for twenty-one and a half years. I felt led by God to do this and asked no questions. I had worked serval jobs while employed there such as a Human Service Worker I (nurse assistant), custodial worker, UTRS, UTRS Supervisor, Dietetic Technician in Food Service and Behavioral Program Specialist.

Sometimes later on that year, God reminded me of the dream I had that Dewayne had gotten shot but in the dream it was at a hotel and I remember daddy calling me on the phone telling me. Well daddy did call me the day of my son murder to tell me the bad news of him being murder. God will warn you before something happen.

My son and I had a distant relationship for a while but a year maybe a year in a half prior to him being murder, we became close again. I really enjoyed the twenty-five years God allowed him to be in my life. Ups and downs are what family have but **LOVE** is stronger than them all.

CHAPTER 20

Living with Pastor

─────────── ❊ ───────────

After being there for several months, found out that the mobile home we were living in was being foreclosed on and we had until September to catch up the payments. Leroy refused to pay any more on the mobile home because he wanted out of the contract. Told Pastor Yvette that I should be paying the mortgage but she didn't agree with him.

Pastor Yvette felt so strongly about us praying and walking the land asking God to intervene on her behalf. We did that religiously and the knock came at the door. The police told us we had to leave the premises and they had to do their jobs. I was on pins and needles knowing we had to go. She asked the officers can they put her belongings in the two car garage and not throw it out in the ditch.

We had to rent a storage to house all our belongings in Hapview. We moved in with her daughter, Rachael and the kids, until October 2006. It was rough sleeping in the room with Pastor Yvette and she kept the television on all night long. The light bothered me and I was unable to get a good night sleep. I would cook, clean, wash or whatever I saw to do, I did.

The three kids were small and Rachael worked, Pastor Yvette and I had to take care of them. As fast as I cleaned up, they messed up. I was grateful for her allowing me to live their because I told Pastor Yvette wherever she went I would go. I just felt that what the Lord wanted me to do. I just wanted to be obedient and lead of the Lord.

CHAPTER 21

Move to Popalock

———————— ❈ ————————

In September of 2006, Pastor Yvette told me she believed the Lord had told her to either move to Truehill or Popalock. I was glad she chose Popalock because that was only four hours away from home.

My daughter, Twanna, had just had my first granddaughter on September 15th and I wanted to be a part of her life. She stayed with my parents at that time. I was there to see her when she had Naomi and able to bathe and care for her while I was there. It was heart-breaking to have to move but I knew God was pleased with my service.

In October of 2006, Pastor Yvette and I moved to Popalock with her sister, Julie. She had closed down the church in Hapview where she pastored.

Pastor Yvette and I were attending an international ministry in Popalock where Pastor Ray was the pastor. After traveling there, we joined and began volunteering in the ministry and neither one of us had jobs.

Pastor Yvette was hired as the kitchen helper for the high school and daycare at the ministry. I would take her Monday-Friday to work from 8 a.m. to 2 p.m. This went on for months. Since we only had the van,

I would stay at the church volunteering in the baby room since they didn't have anybody or aide to take care of the babies.

I would have to be there from 6 a.m. to 6 p.m. most days. There was no one to give me breaks for lunch nor the bathroom. I thought many days to walk away or pull my hair out. Those babies hollered all the time especially Cameron. He cried all day no matter what you did for him. I was so tired daily when we did get home I just barely made it to the couch sitting by the front door. If it was a church night, we just stayed because at 7 p.m. there was church services which was mandatory for us to attend.

Was told in order to get a job at the church, I had to volunteer during church service for daycare, answering phone or wherever else help was needed. I also volunteered in the outreach department. I stocked shelves, gave out food, clothing and signed people in who was served. Finally, I was asked to be the Cook because the cook had resigned in April 2007.

It was a job and Pastor Yvette was to help prepare and serve the food to the daycare. She would only serve while I prepared, cooked, served food as well as shop for it. Some days, I forgot to eat because I was so busy. Being a cook there at the church was hard labor for me. I had to go shopping every two weeks with $700 budget to feed eighty to one hundred people Monday through Friday, breakfast and lunch was very stressful. I had to drive the church van to shop at two stores in which the checks were written out too.

I had to make up menus, order groceries, put up groceries, take inventory, use two kitchens to prepare, prepared report every month of expenditures, cooked breakfast and lunch. Again, I had no help except Pastor Jack served the meals to the daycare once I loaded it on the cart.

At times, I had to walk even in the snow to the trailers to serve breakfast and lunch most of the time. Had to set up sterno, pans, tables, food, utensils, etc. After each meal, I had to clean both kitchens before leaving work. My shift was from 6 a.m. – 2 p.m. but when I had to order groceries, I may not get home until 5 p.m. or later. No overtime was given.

Pastor Ray allowed us to rent his mom three bedroom one bath house minutes away from the church for $750 a month. Two days a week was mandatory to attend church service, volunteer in baby room or answer phone lines during service times. If you were employed by the ministry, you had to attend church services, pay tithes and give your offerings. I had no problem doing either.

While at the ministry, I saw a lot of ministers even the pastor's wife does and say things that was totally wrong. I remember volunteering in the Outreach Ministry where they gave out clothes, food, etc. One Christmas a lady came in to get some clothes, food and we also had toys for the children that was donated.

I would sign them in and give items that Elder Josephine would tell me to give them. This day the lady had been served by giving her meats, groceries, clothes but as she was going out the door, she saw a purse that she liked.

I told her to ask Elder Josephine could she have it but she was rude to the lady. She said, "You haven't thanked me for what I've already given you, no you can't have that purse". I felt so bad for the lady and couldn't understand why she wouldn't allow her to get the purse. It wasn't like she bought it in the first place. All items were donated to the ministry to give out to those in need.

Another time while in church, I had already been working until six that day from six that morning. We had to attend evening service. She found me and told me to go to baby room because they needed someone to see after the babies during service. I did go that day but the very next time she looked for me I hid. She didn't take no mercy on me but would look for me when there were hundreds of others she could ask.

One day it was Pastor Reva birthday and they had sat a big decorated box in front of the church for anyone who wanted to bless her to put it in the box. This particular night, I was in the back where the kitchen was located. After service, I saw her come that way and I wanted to see what she had done. I walked around the corner to see her throwing flowers someone had blessed her with for her birthday in the trash can. That really hurt me for her to not be thankful for the flowers someone probably made a sacrifice just to get for her.

Also I found out an Elder that was very faithful in the ministry was losing her home. Her and husband were faithful and even taught at the bible college. Seems as though the church could have helped with that but didn't really know what happen to the home because soon after we left the ministry.

All last year 2008, God took me through some tremendous changes in my life. In January 2008 on the 25th, I resigned from being a cook at the ministry. I had said to myself earlier that if God tell me to leave, I would. Pastor Paul and Olivia had been coming over to the house to check on us since November 2007. This was the time Pastor Yvette had had an aneurism. Once he was told, he began coming over to our house. This happen after she was released from the hospital. They would call or come by to see what we were in needed.

In December 2007, the van tore up coming off the interstate after coming from seeing Pastor Yvette baby sister. I heard a loud noise coming from under the van. I wanted to pull to the side of road but we were on the interstate. I decided to get off on the exit close to home. The van was shaking so bad that I thought it was going to fall apart.

I got off the interstate to see what was going on and found myself in front of tire place so I pulled into their parking lot. I asked the young woman inside could someone possibly look at it for us and determine what was wrong with it.

When one of the guys became available to look at the van, he pulled it into the stall it. He came where we were sitting along with the young lady and said, "You'll need to get down on you'll knees and thank God". We asked what was going on. She said from the looks and feel of the front wheels, we could have been dead. The tire rod had broken and the wheels were about to come off. We thanked God for his grace and mercy!

We asked what it would cost to get the van fixed. They told us $500 plus dollars. They advised us not to drive it home. Matter of fact, they said that they would be held liable if they allowed us to move it off the premises. I called Mr. Cliff but he was almost home in Popalock. Pastor Yvette told me to call Pastor Paul and he came immediately. When he entered the shop, he told the attendant whatever it cost to fix it, fix it and he took us home.

Around the first part of January 2008, I had dreamt Pastor Paul told me to come off my job. He told Pastor Yvette my dream of Pastor Paul telling me to resign from my job. I told her the dream but I wanted to hear it from him. He did call to tell me to resign. I then put in my two weeks' resignation and left the job.

The next day they called and told us the van was ready. Called Pastor Paul and he came to take me to pick up the van. It cost him over $500 and he wrote a check to pay the amount charged. He followed me home with the van and came back inside. While we were talking he asked us did we want to go home for Christmas. He gave us $300 to go home to Curtail for Christmas.

We were having church in Pastor Paul's home about fifteen of us. The services were powerful and I of course cook for all. We had pastors, prophets, elders and ministers there. Each person got a chance to speak but he was the main speaker. I learned a lot from each of them. God really allowed me to open up more and my voice was heard.

Pastor Paul told us about this million-dollar funding that would come through in February 2008. He wanted us to come under the umbrella, so we did. After receiving my income tax, I paid all house bills and Pastor Yvette and I went shopping, got our hair, nails and new glasses.

The money didn't come through in February but was to come in the middle or latter part of March. Pastor Paul and Olivia told us to leave the house where we were living and to move in with them until the finances comes available. He was going to buy property in Hapview for the ministry, pay off all our bills, pay us a salary, buy us our own brand new vehicles and send us on our way.

Each month thereafter, we waited for the funding to come but never did. We saw him have tantrums when God didn't do what he thought he should do regarding the funding. We had to really pray him through many times. I was aggravated because I couldn't understand why he behaved the way he did.

I saw another side of Pastor Yvette I had never seen. She began teasing and playing with him. When he had mood swings, he would take it out on her. I didn't appreciate nor did I like that. We had a truth table and every time we would sit around the table things began to unfold. I found myself crying and weeping telling Pastor Yvette how she hurt me by things she said and that she wouldn't listen when I tried to be honest with her.

Later, I found out that the spirit in her was intimidating me to stand down when she said things that wasn't true about me that made me feel bad. When I was called a liar by her, it didn't feel good at all. After we went to our rooms, she told me that I didn't have to say that in front of Pastor Paul and Olivia. It was in the open and she didn't appreciate it. I felt even worse after that conversation. I mostly stayed in the room except when cooking, washing or cleaning up.

Even at that, I saw and heard things that was not pleasing. He and Pastor Yvette had like spirits. Both were controlling, selfish and intimidating. It had gotten so bad that she would seldom come down stairs when he was home to keep down confrontation with Pastor Paul.

At the end, I felt Pastor Yvette copped out. She allowed fear to come in her and would not confront Pastor Paul like God had told her to do instead she was ready to go back to Hapview. She decided on August 8th, we were leaving going home. She rented a U-Haul truck and we packed up all our belongings the night before and around midnight, we left going back to Hapview. I was so glad to move back home. Now I can see family again and spend time with my granddaughter.

CHAPTER 22

Moved back to Curtail

───────────── ❈ ─────────────

Moved back to Curtail August 2008. We moved back with her daughter, Rachael and her three children. There was a falling out between the two of them. At that time, I didn't know Pastor Brenda that well but Holy Spirit had told me to contact her. I contacted Pastor Brenda and ask her can Pastor Yvette stay with her until she can find her somewhere to live.

She replied by saying she had to talk with her husband about it and will get back with her. We met with her husband Bishop Matthew and he put Pastor Yvette in a motel for a week. After then, he moved her into their home. Since Pastor Brenda didn't keep house, Pastor Yvette asked if I can stay there for a while to help get their house in order.

At the time, I was staying with my daughter in Borough and her friend. I felt uncomfortable being there in that environment. Sharon called me one day and ask would I stay with her mother while her and Erika her daughter go out of town. That weekend as I was walking outside, I saw in a vision a chariot of fire coming in between Pastor Yvette and I.

I shared the vision with Pastor Yvette and asked her what did it mean. I told her I believe the Lord was telling me it was time for us to separate but she said she didn't think it meant that. I remembered the story of Elijah and Elisha and God let Elisha know that he was going to take Elijah. In order for Elisha minister to begin, Elijah had to be taken.

While I was visiting Pastor Yvette, Bishop Matthew said I can stay there that week helping clean the house. I had my own room and was enjoying it because I didn't have to sleep in room with a television on all night.

I had put in several applications online since August for jobs in Tallahassee because I didn't want to work anymore in Borough. I was talking to Bishop and told him I was applying for jobs. That October I was staying there at the time when I received the phone call from the state department for an interview for Senior Clerk position.

I went in for the interview and it went very well with Mr. William and others. The following week, I got a call to ask did I want the position and when could I began work. That was on a Tuesday when I received the call and I told him that I can start that Friday, October 2008.

Bishop Matthew told me I can continue staying there since I didn't have a car to get to the job. I asked him how much rent would be and he said to just buy things that was needed. He took me to work some days and other days, he allowed me to drive his truck.

When I got paid, I would give Pastor Yvette money and bought things for the house as Bishop instructed me. I would still come home and cook many days, clean, wash and whatever else I seen needed to be done.

A couple months before I had moved into the apartment, Bishop Matthew blessed me with his yellow 1991 Mercedes in church in front of the whole congregation because of my faithfulness to the ministry. He put the keys in my hands in front of the church and it felt good. Now I can drive myself to work, church, around town, pick my children up and bring others to church.

After returning home from church that Sunday, Pastor Yvette was upset because she thought she should have received the car but I knew even if she had gotten the car, I still would have to drive for her.

After Pastor Yvette, talking with me one night saying she was leaving and was I going with her. I told her I needed my own space and she really didn't like that. Stated that I had changed and we don't have the same heart beat anymore.

One day everyone was gone from home except Pastor Yvette. We got home that evening to find Pastor she had left without notice or where she had gone. I felt such a release because I had prayed and ask God to help me because I was afraid to leave or stay. This was God way of releasing me from her after eleven years. She thought I was to continue the journey with her but God had a different plan.

I continued to stay with the Bishop Matthew and Pastor Brenda and also looked for a place to stay of my own. Finally, one day while I was out looking, I was led to an apartment complex in Sunghill. I spoke with the manager on duty and she said they had a special on for the month of June 2009. The special for first month rent free but had to get lights turned on and the key would be mine.

I didn't have money to get lights turned on so she told me where to go get paper to have lights turned on. I went and got paper, took it to light company and lights were turned on. I took the paper back to manager stating lights were on and she gave me key to the two-bedroom apartment.

I only had a container of clothes along with clothes I had purchased since I worked. I was so happy and told Pastor Brenda and Bishop about the apartment. So Bishop told me that they were going to buy me a bedroom suite for my apartment.

I met Pastor Deborah through Bishop Matthew and she told me about this place that gave out furnishings when you move into an apartment but had to be there at 6:00 a.m. They serve you on a first come first serve basis and she took me there. She had a van at the time and we loaded as much as we can. I took home a bedroom set, living room set, cookware and other odds and ends. My apartment was full and I was then able to move in.

My granddaughter, two of my nieces and nephew came over every weekend. We had a good time and I looked forward to seeing them. When I didn't have enough food, I would tell Twanna and Jasper to bring food that weekend.

I was at church every Wednesday, Sunday and other nights and days we had church. The church grew within a year. My granddaughter and two nieces and at that time were the praise team. They enjoyed singing every Sunday and I was so proud of them.

Bishop Matthew would call me daily after I moved out, at work as well as home. He would come by just to talk but mostly to see was there anything he could do to make my life easier. He would sneakily go to my refrigerator as if he wanted something to drink but only wanted to see did I have any groceries.

He would give me money for groceries, gas or just to have in my pocket. Never had met anyone like him especially a man of God. He never made a pass at me. He loved my nieces, nephew and granddaughter. Matter-of- fact, he just loved children altogether.

The entire congregation went with him on speaking engagements to several cities in Curtail, Wayward and Weecha. He always treated us by buying us food and drinks, paying for gas to those who drove their cars. I loved his wife, Pastor Brenda. We became friends and she was like a sister to me.

The church grew so much that we had to move to a bigger building in another location. We had great services and many were ordained in the ministry. We had dancers, singers, ministers, young and old people attending services.

Some time had passed by, I heard the voice of God telling me to stop by this car lot on the way home. So I was telling God how I had a car with no payments and was happy with the Mercedes but I stopped and did what he said.

This particular day, I got out the car just looking at what was on the lot. A young man came out and asked what can he help me with. I told him that I was just looking but wanted a van for my kids and taking people to church. He told me to come inside and discuss some options. Still telling him that I didn't have any money and if I got a vehicle it would be a van.

After talking with him, he asked me could I write a check and he would hold it until I can bring the money. He showed me two vans and since my baby brother wasn't far from there, I asked him to come check out the two vans. I choose the van I wanted, we discussed down payment, payment plan and when I can pick up van.

Payday wasn't until that next week but this dealer took a five hundred dollar check and wrote up another five hundred dollars to match my payment for me to get the van. I asked him was he selling me the van with only two seats in it.

He assured me when I came back on Tuesday, the seats would be in, he will have clean them up and installed them when I come. He was a man of his word and I was now owner of a dodge caravan.

CHAPTER 23

Stranger in My Home

— ❈ —

In September of 2012, Bishop Matthew asked me could I house a young Apostle from Bedrock because he was coming to minister at the church. I had just moved into a four-bedroom home and staying by myself.

I had asked God earlier to bless me with a house to have men and women of God to come to be restored, refreshed and revived. He did as I had asked. So this young man was the first person to enter my home.

I picked the apostle up from the bus station as Bishop Matthew had asked me too. Invited him in my home, gave him a room in back and made him feel at home. My children liked him and even my niece said when we were taking him back to the bus station, after he got out, that the way he looked at me, he was going to be my husband. I took that as a sign.

Bishop Matthew talked to me again about allowing him, the apostle to move in with me and he was to get him a job so he can get his own place. That October, the apostle moved back in hopes to get a job. I had never before let or allowed a single man to move into my home and I was a single female.

Before I had left apartment complex, I had promise Ms. Wilma that she can move in with me because her roommate wanted her out. So Ms. Wilma moved in sometime in November.

The apostle and I had good conversation each night and enjoyed each other company. One day in church Bishop told apostle in front of the congregation that someone there was his wife. I immediately thought Sheri because she needed help with her two children.

To my amaze a couple days later, he told me over the phone that apostle was my husband. I almost flipped out. I believed him because He never would have told me that if it wasn't true. For fourteen long years, I had been celibate. After him telling me that, I saw apostle in a different way. I tried to avoid being in the same room with him. One night, I got so hot I felt as though I was on fire and couldn't hardly contain myself.

CHAPTER 24

Second Marriage

On a Wednesday night, November 8, 2012, the apostle and I talked about marrying. The next day we went to courthouse and got married. I was so excited to finally have a man of God as my husband. God had saved the best for me and I was excited. I failed to consult God about it but believe a **Man**.

Found out George was twelve years younger than I and knew nothing about him except his name and vice versa. Both our families were in awe when we told them. Questions were asked on both sides but couldn't be answered because we didn't have an answer.

Later on that month, Ms. Wilma moved in and room rental papers were signed and dated. It was cool for a while. I was the only one working because it was hard for Apostle to find a job because of his past history.

We had talked about a get together for our families so they could meet us on both sides. Coming up to the gathering, he began telling his family I didn't want them to come down. Stated he wasn't going to be there either when my family arrived. My family did come and we had a good time even though he wasn't there.

Mark and Sue had separated and Bishop asked could Elder Mark rent a room because he was on disability as Ms. Wilma. Everything was going ok for a while. I felt out of place in my own home. When I got home, I still had to cook, wash, clean up because the others mostly stayed in their rooms and my husband was doing his own thing.

Later, Mark asked could Sue, his wife move in and that she was to start work that Tuesday. Found out later that she didn't have a job and then she offered food stamps instead of rent. I accepted it along with George's approval.

The arguments began almost daily before I got home and sometimes while I was home among the husband and wife. Remember one night, I had laid down but couldn't sleep because of the noise. I got up and told them to take it out the door and Mark came up in my face, George stood between us telling him to leave and didn't care where they went but the both of them were to leave.

One day while at work, Ms. Wilma had left to stay with a friend without telling me. She came back to get some clothes while I was at work. The last time she came, my husband told her that she was wrong for not talking with me and needed to take all her stuff with her. She didn't pay rent that month. She left and never came back leaving the rest of her belongings behind.

The constant accusations were daily between the others in the house. Sue wanted to take over while I wasn't there and Jonathan wasn't having it. Finally, after Sue calling the police on my husband, I told her by that Saturday she was to move out and I didn't care where she went and told Mark he can go with her. He took her to the battered women house because she lied to get in. He decided to stay because he had nowhere else to go.

In February 2014, a young lady at church name Delilah asked could her son stay with us for a while she calmed down. Stating that she was going to lay hands on him for talking to her any kind of way and leaving the house without permission.

Delilah wanted to know can her son stay with us for a couple of days because there was two men in house and that they could counsel him in some way to help with his problems. I told her to speak with my husband and Mark since they were both staying there.

She along with Mark and George had a meeting of expectations for her son while he stayed in our home. I was cooking when she arrived and the four of them was in his office with door closed. Therefore, I didn't know what was said nor agreed upon.

One night it was raining, I awake from sleep and went through house checking on everyone. Before I went to bed that night, I told my husband to not leave house, make sure the boy done his homework and for him to call his mom before going to bed by 10 p.m.

The boy was there less than a week. I would make sure he had breakfast, she would pick him up and I would go to work. He was there about a week and she finally told him he could come home.

Mark had spent a lot of time on the phone with Delilah. They would talk nightly while her son stayed there. Sometime she would pick him up from the house months before moved. Mark had moved to Ogre with his mother in June or July 2014 after the boy went back home.

My husband had talked to me about allowing his son, Bryan, to come live with us. He went to pick him up around the last of August or the first of September 2014. Bryan was a quiet young man, stayed to himself and hung out with his dad in office.

In September 2014, my husband went to prison for three years for a crime he stated he didn't commit. During that time, I would visit him in jail and in prison. There were thirty minute visits a day while in jail but once he went to prison, I could stay up to four hours during Saturday visitation.

About two months later, Bryan, moved out without my knowledge and didn't hear from him anymore. I then moved to a two-bedroom trailer because no one lived with me.

Bishop Gabriel took me under his wings along with his wife and nurtured me through the word of God. He introduced me to other leaders such as bishops, prophets, pastors and other Christians in Curtail and Weecha regions.

CHAPTER 25

Led Back to Manscester

————————— ❈ —————————

I felt strongly after about a year in the mobile home to move back to Manscester with my dad. I had to break my two-year lease but my landlord allowed me to do so.

My son, Rodney, moved back to Manscester months before I did. I never wanted to move back there and had told the Lord so many times. After being there for several months, God began to deal with me about why I left Manscester. I was mad with my parents, wanted to move from around them and I did.

Holy Spirit told me I left in the wrong spirit and I needed to confront my issues for leaving. So in August of 2016, I went to daddy along with Rodney as a witness and began to tell him why I left and how I felt.

Told dad how I remembered him being mean to mama and how it really hurt me. Told him of how he would give his truck to my boyfriend, Fred, when I was a teenager to go see other girls. I cried the entire time I was telling him of the things I had held in my heart since I was a teenager. I was then 55 years old.

He told me I should have come to him and talked with him. He admitted being mean to mama and how I held that against him since I was a teenager. He never said he was sorry. Although I didn't hear the answers I wanted, the weight was lifted off my shoulders that day.

In October for 2016, I had dreamt that Angela told me I was going to get disability. I rebuked the dream because I didn't want to be disable having to depend on others.

It hasn't been easy to know mama was out of the house in a nursing home while he was there by himself. Mama and I used to have talks about hoping that she be the longer liver because I didn't know whether or not I could take care of him or wanted to.

Back in the day, daddy done a lot of things I that didn't pleased me but nobody is perfect. He did work and provided for his family. He did have outside children which we were told about at some time.

Retired the following year, February 28, 2017. Still working part time about twenty hours a week with lady pastor daughter and Mr. Joe. They kept me busy for a while. My hours had really dropped dramatically because I couldn't get many hours with the clients I requested.

I was still going back in forth to visit my husband in prison. He appeared to be happy to see me at times and I drove two hours, visited him from eleven to two p.m. each Saturday.

Holy Spirit spoke to me later and told me that being on disability didn't mean I wouldn't be able to take care of myself nor being cripple. I thank God for giving me understanding and received what I had been told. I repented and was forgiven for thinking that way.

Bought me a cash car in June 2017, 2015 Volkswagen Jetta. Took $2000 to fix up Recee house because we were to move in once my husband got out of prison. I painted the house and had rugs put down on the floor. Fred had got bathroom fixed and was only going to charge me but $100 monthly the first year.

He got out of prison in the month July before is birthday. Took him to see the house but he didn't want to live there. I asked dad would it be alright to live with him until we found somewhere to live.

My husband had gained a lot of weight and he didn't feel good about himself. I told him it didn't matter whether he was fat or skinny, I would still love him. He began to go around learning the area and sometimes he would tell me to drop him off in town and walk back home. He didn't realize that it was a long walk from where we lived.

Our relationship wasn't good because of the separation and him never being married. I didn't know how to handle him nor him me. We would talk but at times we both were misunderstood by each other.

In August 2018, I went to court house and got divorce papers, filled them out but didn't go through with it. I showed him the papers so he knew I wasn't playing. We would play cards with my brother and his wife, go shoot pool or walking but I wanted and needed more from him and he refuse me.

He ignored me when I tried to call him when he was out reminding him of time and how I worried about him because he didn't know nobody in the area. After several attempts talking to him about whereabouts and no answering, I told him if he went back to jail or prison I would divorce him.

On December 1, 2018, he went to check in with probation officer and was arrested for violation. I had to get my car from the probation office parking lot. He was sentenced for five months. I went to visit him a couple of times during that period but the conversations were short and brief. I did write him from time to time and put money on the books.

On December 20, 2018, my divorce was finalized. I didn't tell him right away but knew I had too. One day I told him over the phone and he was sad. He said he never wanted the divorce but wanted to be with me until death.

I continue to talk with him and he claim he wanted to remarry me and I agreed with him. I started kind of making some plans but really wanted to see what he was going to do once he was released. He asked my dad over the phone for his permission to marry me. I remember dad saying as long as you treat her right. We both were excited about that. I really felt he meant it!

CHAPTER 26

Fiancé Released

───────────── ❈ ─────────────

Fiancé got out of jail in 2018 the day before we were to funeralized mama. Family had come from out of town gathering at the house. George was walking in and out of house, wasn't speaking to anyone nor having conversation except on his phone.

My brother, Ben, got upset with George being disrespectful by not speaking and walking all over him. He and his wife left because of what had happen. They were to stay the night. I felt as though I was caught in the middle. I was grieving my mom too. He apologized to him but it aggravated me because he was cursing on the phone.

That night I was really hurting and my fiancé just held me in his arms. He really comforted me and went to funeral with me the next day. He knew how to comfort me at times but it didn't last long. He was there for me during the loss of my mother and I really, really appreciated him for being there.

George got a job working at a Lumber Company not long after returning home. I can see the change in him once he got money in hand. He only wanted to please himself and never wanted to contribute to the house. I did get a car for him so he could drive himself to work.

He began buying all sorts of things such as jewelry, clothes etc. but not giving me anything. He did buy me a wedding ring but after a disagreement one night, I gave it back to him. He threw it on the floor, the next day went back to the store and got his money back. That was very disappointing because he didn't even attempt to want to give it back to me.

He was gone more and I was concern about his whereabouts. At times, he wouldn't answer when I called him. He was new to the area and had no family here so I was scared and worried about him being alright or coming home at a decent time.

We had planned on getting remarried in July 2018 but the closer it got to the date red flags kept coming up in my spirit. On the day of my bridal shower, I told everyone that attended that I called off the wedding and was sorry for wasting their time.

I just couldn't see myself going back into a no win situation when I considered my happiness. I am not perfect but I deserve better. I weighed out the options and the option of not remarrying was the best decision I've made in a long time.

George son had taken time off to come to be in the wedding but due to the cancellation, he still wanted to come. Ann and I drove to Bayou to bring him home to Manscester.

His dad and him had a good time hanging out together. I made sure he had good hot meals each day and we hung out a little too. His dad worked night shift so he wasn't able to spend a lot of time with him but when they did, they enjoyed each other.

George turned into another person when he and his son was together. After coming here, his son had bad news that his best friend, cousin had been murder so he was down for a bit. I tried to encourage him as much as I could. His son was such a jewel, well manner and loved his dad.

Ann and I took him back to Bayou, would do it all again if I had too. He was just a nice young man. I prayed for him and wanted him to succeed in whatever he puts his mind too.

Since we weren't getting married and he was sharing a house with me and my dad, I ask God to let him find a place to stay or for a door to open whereas he can move out. God allowed an ex-sister-in-law to call one day telling me about this house in Pleasanthill.

I told him about it and he got excited so when he came home that morning, we went to see the house. The house had great potential and we can work it but I didn't have a full time job and had retired. He could have paid the $500 rent each month and with my working periodically, we could have made it work.

We called the guy and he met with us there. Told us he would get the papers drawn up and to meet him at his house for the signing. He requested $1,000 down and we signed the papers, him and I.

I was told by my sister-in-law that she overheard my fiance' talking and saying that would only be his house and he didn't want me there. I never confronted him about it but just was glad he had somewhere to go. The guy who we sign papers with also told me that the day of the signing, George, was acting suspicious. I knew God had open this door to get him out the house from with my dad and me.

The house set way back off the road. Three bedroom, two bathrooms, dining room, kitchen and living room. Before he moved there, we had painted inside and outside getting it ready for move in. I was only to move there if we remarry.

One day while we were painting the house, I sat on the couch in the living room. I heard the Holy Spirit say "this is not your house". I got up went outside, walked around in yard crying to myself. When he asked me what I was doing, I just said I'm just walking around in the yard.

The last of August 2018, George moved in a house we had both signed to rent to own. He had mentioned earlier that he needed roommates to help with the bills there. He then had three people to move there with him.

September 8, 2018, around 3 a.m. I received a call from him saying I needed to come to the house. I didn't know what I was going into and was a little scared. I prayed the whole way there because I didn't know what I was going into. I had a crack in my window asking him what was going on.

A roommate and him had had an argument but didn't understand what had happened. He had told the young man to leave but he wouldn't. He had already called the police. Once the police arrived, they began questioning him as to what was going on and then asked for both of their identification.

They told George, there was a warrant for his arrest, handcuffed him and took him to jail. Yet again I was disappointed in him, didn't even go to his sentencing but was told he was going to prison for two years. I stayed mad with him for a while not even wanting to talk with him.

After him going back to prison, the gentleman in whom we had signed papers for the house called me. I told him what had happen and that I couldn't pay the house note. I was supposed to work for his daughter but her facility didn't open up; therefore, I couldn't pay rent without a job. We agreed that he would sell the house and he already had a buyer. We met and paper was annulled and the house was sold. God allowed me to get out of that house and didn't cost me anything. God protects his own because he only wants the best for us.

In October of 2018, I had a dream and in it God showed me a man and said that was my husband. I rebuked the dream because he was in church of God in Christ. To me these people still had church like back in the day and wasn't open to new things.

As I pondered on the dream, I said Lord not my will but your will be done. I strongly believe his word when he says, "he will give us the desires of our heart", Psalm 34:4. I also thought of another verse which says "he will not hold any good thing from his children", Psalm 84:11.

CHAPTER 27

Year 2019

In June 2019, I lost my 2013 Volkswagen Jetta because I had gotten a payday loan and wasn't able to pay it off. I was very distraught because before then the air went out in my car, had two clients that I had to give up.

I then took the car to an air conditioner place and they said the compressor was gone in it. That's when I went to the title loan place to borrow the money to get it fixed. I wasn't having the clients I needed to make the monthly payments or pay the loan back, so I lost it.

I was disappointed in myself not counting up the cost and that I had made a stupid mistake, again. I told two friends of mine what I had done, was unable to pay and car was taken as a repo. This one friend had gotten a large amount of money for her retirement and could had loan it to me but she didn't. For about two weeks, she had asked me how much it cost to get the car back. By that time, I was disgusted and disappointed because I knew she could have helped but didn't.

Now I was without a car and a job. For three months, I stayed home except for church and grocery shopping. I had to borrow cars or pay someone to for taking me both places. I was very disappointed because every time I asked my brother to take me to town, I paid him. It was several times in the past, that I allowed him along with other family members to use my car and never ask for gas nor money.

In June 2019, I went before the disability court. I knew that the Lord had told me I would be getting disability. By the end of August, I was told my disability was approved. My back time of six months was put in my account in middle of September. God had done it again! I remembered the dream in the latter part of 2017 when he told me through Angela that I was going out on disability.

I took some of the money, went to car lot and paid down on my daughter, Twanna, a truck of her liking. I thank God that I was able to do that for my daughter. She has always looked out for her mama when I needed her. She would keep my hair up, buy food for my house and give me money when I asked.

God allowed me to pay her truck off within a year and I thank him for it. My daughter and granddaughter now have a safe vehicle that don't break down and leave them stranded beside the road.

Now since I'm on the Lord side, I do ministry in different areas, have a church home, feeding, cooking, loving on others, travel different places and am pumped for my Lord and savior. I am now living my best life and know who I am and whose I am. My life is to live life to the fullest by doing the will of my father, Jesus Christ and holy spirit.

CHAPTER 28

Words of Encouragement

---✦---

Just remember you too are somebody special to God. Trials, tests and troubles may come but God will deliver us from them all. I am foremost thankful to God for allowing me to know that I am somebody in him and life circumstances can change with having a personal relationship with God the father, God the Son and God the Holy Spirit.

My life has taken a tremendous turn around all for the best. Just remember somebody have gone through more trauma than you and they came out.

You are never alone in this world and know that you have a heavenly father who loves you and looks out for you every day.

A changed mind about life in general and how God prizes us makes a difference. A changed mind **will** change your world. Focus on the good and never the bad. Keep a positive attitude about life situations. There is better for you!

Nothing is never as bad as it seems but without God, you wouldn't know that. Hang out with Jesus and let him direct your path. He wants what's best for his children and guess what, *you are one of his children*.

God has no respect of persons and if he did it for me, surely he will do it for you. Stop letting the world and Satan dictate with the things that will only bring you temporary happiness but lean on God who will give you eternal things. Lean not on your own understanding and in all your ways trust God. It is never as bad as it seems.

Know your worth and never settle for anything less. Blessings to you and again, thank you for taking the time out to read my story. Can't tell it all but know that I love you and God loves you most!!!!

Printed in the United States
by Baker & Taylor Publisher Services